breathe.
a guided healing journal for black men

brennan allan steele

First Printing, 2020

Cover Design by Aaron Tucker – aarontuckerdesigner.myportfolio.com
Author Photo by Chandler Phillips – chandlerphillips.co

ISBN 978-0-578-73935-9

intro.

I watched him die. I watched him as the knee of white supremacy took his life from him. I watched him pass into eternity as the cries of his mortality fell on deaf ears by a man and a system that devalued his humanity.

As a black man in America, I've been conditioned to understand the fragility of my existence in a society that sees it as dispensable. From Emmett Till to Trayvon Martin, I've seen, learned, and heard firsthand that I am not important to a world not built for me.

But, watching George Floyd's death did something different to me. I don't know if it was the grief from a never-ending attack against black bodies, the added pressure of being amidst a global health pandemic with COVID-19, or the fact that I literally watched the slow agony of life leaving him. Regardless, the days and weeks following were an emotional roller coaster. I felt numb or angry much of the time, but I also felt a sense of deep sadness and even fear that I could be next.

Still, many of my emotions went unprocessed. Growing up, I struggled to find the space to process my emotions openly. Both the expectations of my manhood to be without emotion and the weight of carrying the societal tropes of a black man have prevented me from fully being free to process, heal, understand, and grow.

After the initial days of my personal turmoil surrounding George Floyd's death, I started to reflect on how many other black men were experiencing what I was. How many other black men had unprocessed emotions and trauma? How many other black men have had life stories stifled by the narratives surrounding their identity?

After reflection, wrestling, and prayer around those notions, the idea for this journal developed. Though processing who we are verbally may be difficult for many of us, I've found that journaling can do so much to help us to at least have somewhere to start.

So, I hope this journal gives you space and catalyzes your healing, brother.

The Game Plan

Breathing, as a black man, is an act of resistance. Every day you breathe, every day you wear your crown, and every day you shine your light, you threaten to stun the world around you.

This journal will be both therapeutic and sharpening for you. At the end of this 45-day journey, you will have a better awareness of who you are, where you've been, and where you're going. You will be able to breathe easier and stronger.

A Three-Part Journey:

Part One: The first 30 days of the journal are guided. You will have specific topics, prompts, and activities to get you started with journaling, reflecting, and processing.

Part Two: The next 14 days will be a self-directed journal, with mostly free space for you to continue thinking about topics in the first part or exploring other topics that the journey has brought up for you.

Part Three: This part is all about claiming and writing your own story and narrative.

Key Features:

You Good, Bruh? - This is a daily check-in tool. Being able to articulate how you feel is vital to knowing yourself fully.

Exhale - Here you will have space to explain the emotion(s) selected in detail.

Release Point: This is a curated definition of the topic or focus of the day. Important pieces of the definition are highlighted and meant to help you center yourself for the daily activity.

part one

guided journal.

For the first thirty days of this journal, you will work through a set of writing prompts, exercises, and reflection questions that focus on one of three topics that are denoted in the Release Point section each day. Those three focus areas you will cycle through are:

1. *Self*: These entries will help you understand your life story both as it has been written thus far and how you want to write it in the future.

2. *Identity:* To make this journal relevant to you, these entries will create space for you to explore some of the pieces of your journey that are unique to you as a black man.

3. *EQ*: This acronym is short for emotional intelligence. These entries will help you gain a better understanding of yourself through reflection on the good, the bad, and the ugly of your emotions

Here's to a new journey of self-exploration, explicitly designed specifically for you, brother.

You Good, Bruh?

What emotion(s) are you feeling today? Circle them.

Joyful	Neutral	Anxious
Grateful	Numb	Fearful
Motivated	Sad	Guilty
Hopeful	Tired	Angry
Content	Stressed	Other: __________

Exhale

List up to three reasons (or interactions or thoughts) why you're feeling the emotion(s):

1. ______________________________

2. ______________________________

3. ______________________________

Release Point

Here is today's focus and curated definition.

self

narrative

/ˈnerədiv/ *noun*

1. a written account of a series of related events
2. a story
3. the representation of a situation that conforms to a predetermined set of aims, beliefs, and values

narrative

Writing YOUR Life Story

#TrayvonMartin #EricGarner #PhilandoCastile #AmaudArberry #GeorgeFloyd #RayshardBrooks

Too many of our brothers have been reduced to hashtags and their life stories have been at the mercy of the narratives of the racist society that killed them. Let's reclaim your story, brother. Use today's activity to help you get started. At the end of this journey, you'll have a chance to write your full story.

---

1. Where'd it all start for you? Briefly describe your family of origin, where you're from, and where your journey began.

2. Where are you now? Describe what's going on in your life right now.

3. Use the circles below to fill-in as many impactful moments in your life that you can remember that were integral in getting you from where you started to where you are now. Include the good, the bad, and the ugly.

You Good, Bruh?

What emotion(s) are you feeling today? Circle them.

Joyful	Neutral	Anxious
Grateful	Numb	Fearful
Motivated	Sad	Guilty
Hopeful	Tired	Angry
Content	Stressed	Other: ________

Exhale

List up to three reasons (or interactions or thoughts) why you're feeling the emotion(s):

1. ______________________________

2. ______________________________

3. ______________________________

Release Point

Here is today's focus and curated definition.

identity

identity

/ˌīˈden(t)ədē/ *noun*

1. the characteristics that define a person
2. how a person sees themselves
3. the way the world views a person

Being a Black Man

If you are completing the journey of this journal, you likely identify as a black man. This identity marker has been a source of pride for some and fear for others. It is a source of unity for those who wear it and a source of intimidation for those who do not. Yet, "black man" is not worn monolithically, and as such, should be explored by the individual.

This is your space to start to unpack how you personally operate in your own masculinity in the context of your race. There is no one "right" way to be a black man, despite how it may seem. As you answer today's questions, feel free to also explore how other parts of your identity intersect with your black masculinity.

---

1. What does it mean to you to be a black man?

2. Where or from whom did you learn how to be a black man?

3. How do you choose to show up in this identity? How do you wear your black masculinity?
   (For example: My black masculinity shows up in the way that I relate to the world around me. As a teacher of black boys, I present my black masculinity as strong, sensitive, intelligent, resilient, and able to have the best comebacks to their jokes.)

day three

You Good, Bruh?

What emotion(s) are you feeling today? Circle them.

Joyful	Neutral	Anxious
Grateful	Numb	Fearful
Motivated	Sad	Guilty
Hopeful	Tired	Angry
Content	Stressed	Other: __________

Exhale

List up to three reasons (or interactions or thoughts) why you're feeling the emotion(s):

1. ______________________________

2. ______________________________

3. ______________________________

Release Point

Here is today's focus and curated definition.

eq

joy

/joi/ *noun*

1. great pleasure and enduring happiness
2. delight
3. an emotion caused by well-being, confidence, or assurance

Cultivate Joy

My therapist always says, "On the other side of healing is joy." As I do the hard work of healing from the wounds in my story that thought motivates me. Yet, even before full healing is attained, you can cultivate joy in your life if you are intentional about it. Joy has the ability to be the counteractive force against the heaviness of the burdens you carry, brother.

In the activity below, first write your definition of joy. Then, in the boxes, write down the things that specifically help you experience #blackboyjoy. What makes you smile? Is it an activity? A sport? Being around certain people? Whatever it is, write it down.

What does joy mean to you?

My Joy Definition:

Fill in the boxes below with some of the things that bring you joy.

When the weight of the world tries to get you down, you can refer back here and prioritize the things that give you joy.

day four

You Good, Bruh?

What emotion(s) are you feeling today? Circle them.

Joyful	Neutral	Anxious
Grateful	Numb	Fearful
Motivated	Sad	Guilty
Hopeful	Tired	Angry
Content	Stressed	Other: __________

Exhale

List up to three reasons (or interactions or thoughts) why you're feeling the emotion(s):

1. ______________________________

2. ______________________________

3. ______________________________

Release Point

Here is today's focus and curated definition.

self

assertion

/ə'sərSH(ə)n/ *noun*

1. a confident statement of belief
2. a positive declaration
3. a proclamation

assertion

"I AM A MAN"

In 1968, sanitation workers in Memphis took to the street to strike in response to the denial of their basic civil rights as black workers. Their rallying cry was "I AM A MAN." This was a simple statement, but acutely declared and centered these men's humanity in a racist society.

Brother, in a world that attempts to define your existence and truncate the magnificence of who you are into stereotypes, tropes, and caricatures, there is often little space for you to define yourself. So, I ask you, Black man, how do you describe yourself?

Fill in the "I AM" statements below to describe yourself. This may be difficult at first because you may have rarely been given space to define yourself. If you're stuck, you can list characteristics about yourself, talk about the roles you play in other people's lives, or just who you hope to be. For example, I would say "I AM resilient" or "I AM emotionally healthy."

Describe YOURSELF, Brother.
TEN ASSERTIONS

#1: I AM ______________________

#2: I AM ______________________

#3: I AM ______________________

#4: I AM ______________________

#5: I AM ______________________

#6: I AM ______________________

#7: I AM ______________________

#8: I AM ______________________

#9: I AM ______________________

#10: I AM ______________________

You Good, Bruh?

What emotion(s) are you feeling today? Circle them.

Joyful	Neutral	Anxious
Grateful	Numb	Fearful
Motivated	Sad	Guilty
Hopeful	Tired	Angry
Content	Stressed	Other: __________

Exhale

List up to three reasons (or interactions or thoughts) why you're feeling the emotion(s):

1. ______________________________

2. ______________________________

3. ______________________________

Release Point

Here is today's focus and curated definition.

identity

blackness

/ˈblaknəs/ *noun*

1. the state of belonging to a people group with more melanin
2. used to describe the experience of people with a shared history of oppression socio-politically
3. the celebration of beauty

Black Is...

I was always taught that this world was stacked against people who looked like me. It wasn't until college that I truly started to take pride in my blackness. Unlike me, some of you may have grown up in a family that taught you to take pride in your blackness. Others of you may have understood your blackness through the hatred and discomfort from peers. Regardless, your coming-of-age and your becoming was impacted by it.

Answer the questions below as you reflect on your initial consciousness of your blackness. If you don't remember the first moment you encountered your blackness, try to think of the earliest moment you can. Try not to put on value-judgment on how substantive your experience is. It is your story.

---

1. Recount the moment when you realized you were black.

2. What emotions did this moment cause or bring up?

3. How did this moment affect your view of your race as you grew up?

You Good, Bruh?

What emotion(s) are you feeling today? Circle them.

Joyful	Neutral	Anxious
Grateful	Numb	Fearful
Motivated	Sad	Guilty
Hopeful	Tired	Angry
Content	Stressed	Other: __________

Exhale

List up to three reasons (or interactions or thoughts) why you're feeling the emotion(s):

1. ______________________________

2. ______________________________

3. ______________________________

Release Point

Here is today's focus and curated definition.

eq

fear

/'fir/ noun, verb

1. an emotion caused by potential pain, harm, or threat
2. to be scared or afraid
3. a feeling of anxiety at an anticipated outcome

Owning Your Fears

Everything around you may tell you that fear is not an emotion you can exhibit or process. Between the expectations of your manhood and the fear that is directed toward you by people who judge the color of your skin, your own fears likely have been overtaken. Yet, they still exist and prevent you from reaching your potential. One step to overcoming fears is acknowledging, and owning, them.

You may say, "I don't fear anything." While this may be true, challenge yourself to think deeply about what worries you, concerns you, or even scares you, as you answer the today's questions, brother. Fears are not uncommon; it's when we let them fester that they can be damaging.

---

1. What is your biggest fear?

2. When do you fear it most?

3. Why do you fear it?

You Good, Bruh?

What emotion(s) are you feeling today? Circle them.

Joyful	Neutral	Anxious
Grateful	Numb	Fearful
Motivated	Sad	Guilty
Hopeful	Tired	Angry
Content	Stressed	Other: ________

Exhale

List up to three reasons (or interactions or thoughts) why you're feeling the emotion(s):

1. ____________________
2. ____________________
3. ____________________

Release Point

Here is today's focus and curated definition.

self

dream
/drēm/ *noun, verb*

1. a fantasy, aspiration, or ambition
2. indulging in the seemingly implausible
3. considering the possibility of doing something or the occurrence of something

Deferred Dreams

Black men aren't often allowed to dream. Many of us don't remember dreaming since we were boys, and even then, it was likely stymied by the realities of our existence. As Langston Hughes wrote, our dreams were deferred by the conditions of a society not built for us to be able to freely dream. But today I challenge you to dream, brother. No matter your stage in life, reigniting the ability to dream is a form of inner liberation.

In the clouds below, respond to the prompt given. This question is left intentionally broad for you to take in the direction you want. These dreams can be related to a set of uninhibited goals, a future version of yourself, a vision of radical change in some area you're passionate about, or anything else. This is your journal, brother.

What are your *wildest* dreams?

You Good, Bruh?

What emotion(s) are you feeling today? Circle them.

Joyful	Neutral	Anxious
Grateful	Numb	Fearful
Motivated	Sad	Guilty
Hopeful	Tired	Angry
Content	Stressed	Other: __________

Exhale

List up to three reasons (or interactions or thoughts) why you're feeling the emotion(s):

1. ______________________________

2. ______________________________

3. ______________________________

Release Point

Here is today's focus and curated definition.

identity

stereotype

/ ˈsterēəˌtīp/ *noun*

1. a widely held oversimplified ideal of a person
2. baseless and generalized view of a person or people group
3. a box that one is expected fit into

Two Strikes

My momma always taught me that I had at least two strikes against me: being Black and being a Black man. It's likely that you also had a similar experience with your parents. Ultimately, our black parents and families have taught us this since we were young to protect and warn. As such, when moments of racial trauma occur, they are taken as part of the status quo, seldom to be processed. Unprocessed trauma prevents true healing. So, here's your chance, brother.

As you answer the question below, resist the urge to just write about these moments descriptively, as to distance yourself. If you can, take yourself back to those moments and sit in them. Describe the situation and all of the emotions you can give voice to.

Reflect on 1-2 (or more) moments when you have been stereotyped or discriminated against because of your identity. What happened and how did those instances make you feel?

You Good, Bruh?

What emotion(s) are you feeling today? Circle them.

Joyful	Neutral	Anxious
Grateful	Numb	Fearful
Motivated	Sad	Guilty
Hopeful	Tired	Angry
Content	Stressed	Other: ________

Exhale

List up to three reasons (or interactions or thoughts) why you're feeling the emotion(s):

1. ______________________________

2. ______________________________

3. ______________________________

Release Point

Here is today's focus and curated definition.

eq

gratitude

/ ˈgradəˌt(y)o͞od/ *noun*

1. the quality of thankfulness
2. an emotion or mood of appreciation
3. a heart posture

A Grateful Heart

One of the easiest ways to look at the world around you is through a lens of darkness. There's surely enough darkness and despair around us globally, nationally, and even in our personal lives. For today though, I want you to focus on the light in your life, brother. Developing a heart of gratitude can shift your mindset, centering your mind on what really matters and the good in your life. A mindset shift can go a long way towards lasting joy.

Make a list of the first 15 things that come to mind that you are grateful for. You can include whatever you want: people, places, things, experiences, and the like.

1. ______________________________
2. ______________________________
3. ______________________________
4. ______________________________
5. ______________________________
6. ______________________________
7. ______________________________
8. ______________________________
9. ______________________________
10. ______________________________
11. ______________________________
12. ______________________________
13. ______________________________
14. ______________________________
15. ______________________________

Pick three of those things on your gratitude list that you are particularly grateful for and answer the questions below.

1. Write down your choices
   #1:____

   #2:____

   #3:____

2. Why are you grateful for what you listed in #1? Be specific.

3. Why are you grateful for what you listed in #2? Be specific.

4. Why are you grateful for what you listed in #3? Be specific.

You Good, Bruh?

What emotion(s) are you feeling today? Circle them.

Joyful	Neutral	Anxious
Grateful	Numb	Fearful
Motivated	Sad	Guilty
Hopeful	Tired	Angry
Content	Stressed	Other: ________

Exhale

List up to three reasons (or interactions or thoughts) why you're feeling the emotion(s):

1. ______________________________

2. ______________________________

3. ______________________________

Release Point

Here is today's focus and curated definition.

self

superpower
/ ˈso͞opərˌpou(ə)r/ *noun*

1. a power possessed by superheroes
2. a special ability that is unique to you
3. an asset that allows you bring your best and give your best to every situation

Uniquely Equipped

Black Panther is my favorite superhero because he represents what I know to be true about black men. We are strong, brilliant, and resilient. We are kings. You, as a black man, bring something beautiful to this world. You have something inside you that the world needs, and there is something that you do better than anyone else in the world. What is that marvelous thing, brother?

Use today's questions to reflect on your superpower. If you are struggling with this, you can ask your loved ones what they appreciate the most about you, what you are passionate about, or you can take the time to reflect on how you normally contribute to teams and problem-solving. I know you've got something special.

---

1. What's your superpower? Write it in the bubble below!

2. When is your superpower most useful and apparent?

3. Are there any areas of your life where you aren't utilizing your superpower, or it isn't being respected? If so, in what areas can you do more to make sure your unique abilities are being exercised and honored?

day eleven

You Good, Bruh?

What emotion(s) are you feeling today? Circle them.

Joyful	Neutral	Anxious
Grateful	Numb	Fearful
Motivated	Sad	Guilty
Hopeful	Tired	Angry
Content	Stressed	Other: ________

Exhale

List up to three reasons (or interactions or thoughts) why you're feeling the emotion(s):

1. ______________________________

2. ______________________________

3. ______________________________

Release Point

Here is today's focus and curated definition.

identity

confidence

/ 'känfədəns/ *noun*

1. a feeling of certainty about a specific truth
2. a disposition of self-assurance in one's characteristics
3. a positive outlook of oneself

Love Yo'self

You may have had the thought at some point that being a black man is tiring. I wouldn't blame you for feeling fatigued or even shame because of the messages the world gives us. But I want to challenge you to have confidence in being a black man, brother. Being a black man is not tiring; living in a society with white supremacy built into its fabric is. Let's create more positive energy around our identity.

Use today's entry to counter the narratives that you have been socialized to believe about your own identity. You are not a threat. You are not a criminal. You are not a thug.

Set a timer for 5 minutes. In that time, think about all the things you love about being a black man. You can put it in list form or take an abstract approach. The space on this and the next page are left blank for that reason intentionally.

What do you ***love*** about being a black man?

Continue with the self-love on this page, brother.

You Good, Bruh?

What emotion(s) are you feeling today? Circle them.

Joyful	Neutral	Anxious
Grateful	Numb	Fearful
Motivated	Sad	Guilty
Hopeful	Tired	Angry
Content	Stressed	Other: __________

Exhale

List up to three reasons (or interactions or thoughts) why you're feeling the emotion(s):

1. ____________________

2. ____________________

3. ____________________

Release Point

Here is today's focus and curated definition.

eq

sadness

/ ˈsadnəs/ *noun*

1. a feeling caused by unhappiness
2. an emotional pain resulting from grief or loss
3. a demonstration of sorrow

Mourning Time

We have all had experiences that have led to deep sadness, grief, or a sense of loss. These experiences can be anything from the loss of a loved one to the loss of the life you thought you'd have. Grief is a part of the human experience, but it can wreak havoc if not acknowledged or left unprocessed. How we respond to grief and sadness can also teach us a lot about ourselves.

While answering the questions below, reflect on a moment of deep sadness and grief. As you do this, embrace the discomfort of sitting in that moment. If it helps, take some time to relive that moment. Once you finish today's entry, take some space for yourself. Refer back to your 'joy' entry and do one of the things you listed.

---

1. Describe the moment of deep sadness or grief. Try to use as much detail as possible.

2. What about the experience caused you sadness or grief?

3. How did you respond to feelings of sadness or grief in the moment? Why?

4. How does it feel to relive that moment now? Why?

You Good, Bruh?

What emotion(s) are you feeling today? Circle them.

Joyful	Neutral	Anxious
Grateful	Numb	Fearful
Motivated	Sad	Guilty
Hopeful	Tired	Angry
Content	Stressed	Other: ________

Exhale

List up to three reasons (or interactions or thoughts) why you're feeling the emotion(s):

1. ______________________________

2. ______________________________

3. ______________________________

Release Point

Here is today's focus and curated definition.

self

value

/ˈvalyo͞o/ *noun*

1. what a **person decides** is important in life
2. **guiding principles** for decisions and behavior
3. ideals **held in high regard**

Values Alignment

Black man, the more you understand yourself, the more you can be healthy, strong, and able to affect change in your family and community. Yet, it is hard to have vision, goals, or a path for your life without being clear on what you value. Knowing your values allows you to have a barometer to check and make sure that all of your actions and decisions are aligned with those values.

Today, you will be exploring your values. One way to figure out your values if you do not already know them is to first reflect on a couple of moments where you felt like you were your best self or at the top of the world. What about those moments gave those positive feelings? If this doesn't work, see the reference section on page 94 for guidance.

What are your top 3 values?

#1: ______________ #2: ______________ #3: ______________

Use the organizers below to think through your values more specifically.

Value #1: __________________

Why is this one of your values?	
In what aspects of your life does this value show up most often?	In what aspects of your life is the value not present or prioritized?

Value #2: ___________________

Why is this one of your values?	
In what aspects of your life does this value show up most often?	In what aspects of your life is the value not present or prioritized?

Value #3: ___________________

Why is this one of your values?	
In what aspects of your life does this value show up most often?	In what aspects of your life is the value not present or prioritized?

You Good, Bruh?

What emotion(s) are you feeling today? Circle them.

Joyful	Neutral	Anxious
Grateful	Numb	Fearful
Motivated	Sad	Guilty
Hopeful	Tired	Angry
Content	Stressed	Other: __________

Exhale

List up to three reasons (or interactions or thoughts) why you're feeling the emotion(s):

1. ______________________________

2. ______________________________

3. ______________________________

Release Point

Here is today's focus and curated definition.

identity

community
/ kə'myo͞onədē/ *noun*

1. the friends, family, and other people who one spends time with
2. a source of accountability and comradery
3. the homies, ride-or-dies, or squad

True Brotherhood

Growing up, I often found that my deepest relationships were never usually with men, especially not other black men. While I was often able to share and be vulnerable with women in my life, conversations with the men in my life were limited to sports, significant others, music, or anything else surface-level to avoid seeming "weak" or "soft."

However, in adulthood I've realized that an authentic community with other brothers is an integral piece of my well-being and development. I've discovered that when other men are vulnerable with me, it invites me to be vulnerable in kind and produces more meaningful relationships where I feel more known and seen by someone who "gets it.'

You need to maintain a level of vulnerability with your bruhs, bros, brothas-from-other-mothas, or whatever you call them, brother.

Use this entry to reflect on that state your current community. If you don't have any guy friends, use today to reflect on what has prevented you from having them. Go a step further and identify guys in your life that have potential homie status.

---

1. Who in your community, regardless of gender, are you most open and vulnerable with? Why? (This can be anyone, including family members.)

2. Who are your brothers (guy friends)?

3. What topics are easy to talk about with them? Why?

4. What topics are difficult to talk about with them? Why?

5. If there were no risks, what personal matters would you share with them and seek their counsel on?

Challenge: Share what you wrote in #5 with your brothers the next time you chill with them.

You Good, Bruh?

What emotion(s) are you feeling today? Circle them.

Joyful	Neutral	Anxious
Grateful	Numb	Fearful
Motivated	Sad	Guilty
Hopeful	Tired	Angry
Content	Stressed	Other: __________

Exhale

List up to three reasons (or interactions or thoughts) why you're feeling the emotion(s):

1. ______________________________

2. ______________________________

3. ______________________________

Release Point

Here is today's focus and curated definition.

eq

anger

/ 'aNGgər/ *noun*

1. an emotion expressed as a result of annoyance or displeasure
2. a healthy, human emotion
3. a feeling in reaction to a wrong, injustice, or evil

Understand Your Anger

Anger might be a common emotion for you. As boys, we are often taught that anger is an acceptable emotion as opposed to sadness or fear. Otherwise, if you're like me, it may be an emotion that you are scared to emote because you don't want to confer stereotypes or risk being angry at the wrong place or time. Either way, you have a right to be angry, and as with all emotions, your anger should be explored and understood.

Take your time and answer each of today's questions fully. While anger is your right, it could be detrimental to you and others if it shows up in unhealthy ways. You may use a specific incident to reflect on this if that is helpful.

---

1. What makes you angry?

2. How do you express your anger?

3. How does your anger affect those around you?

4. Do you feel that you demonstrate your anger in healthy or unhealthy ways? Why or why not?

You Good, Bruh?

What emotion(s) are you feeling today? Circle them.

Joyful	Neutral	Anxious
Grateful	Numb	Fearful
Motivated	Sad	Guilty
Hopeful	Tired	Angry
Content	Stressed	Other: __________

Exhale

List up to three reasons (or interactions or thoughts) why you're feeling the emotion(s):

1. ______________________________

2. ______________________________

3. ______________________________

Release Point

Here is today's focus and curated definition.

self

kryptonite

/ˈkriptəˌnīt/ *noun*

1. a substance that inhibits Superman's powers
2. something that weakens or harms a person
3. a threat to overall strength that could lead to one's downfall

kryptonite

Guarding Against Weakness

Despite his superpowers, Superman is rendered almost useless when he comes in contact with kryptonite. Brother, everyone has a weakness. Perhaps, you don't like to admit your weakness because it threatens your manhood. Or maybe it's something that you wouldn't identify as a weakness, but it gets you off your game, negatively affecting you and those around you. Moreover, our weaknesses have the effect they do because we continue to entertain them or indulge in them, even after we have clearly identified them.

Today is about identifying those weaknesses and then taking steps to guard against them. Dig deep and be honest with yourself here.

---

1. What is your kryptonite?

2. When are you most susceptible to it negatively affecting you?

3. How do you make space for your kryptonite to continue to have an impact on you?

4. What steps can you take to guard yourself against your kryptonite?

You Good, Bruh?

What emotion(s) are you feeling today? Circle them.

Joyful	Neutral	Anxious
Grateful	Numb	Fearful
Motivated	Sad	Guilty
Hopeful	Tired	Angry
Content	Stressed	Other: __________

Exhale

List up to three reasons (or interactions or thoughts) why you're feeling the emotion(s):

1. ______________________________

2. ______________________________

3. ______________________________

Release Point

Here is today's focus and curated definition.

identity

trauma

/ˈtroumə/ *noun*

1. a distressful event
2. emotional shock caused by a direct or indirect experience that affects one's personhood
3. an event, or series of events that has sustained negative impact on one's well-being

Acknowledging Racial Trauma

We live in a society where physical attacks on black bodies have not been uncommon since its inception. Witnessing the brutal death of people that look like us, whether it be lynching or police brutality, almost seems to be a normal part of black existence. Yet, it is *not normal* for you to witness, watch, or hear about unarmed men with the same demographics as you shot and killed. Experiencing this is traumatic and should be processed as such.

You may not have had the space or ability to really understand the impact of this trauma on you. Here's your chance, brother. As you complete today's entry, make sure to push beyond feelings of anger and shock. Take time to sit with how it has impacted the way you carry yourself, interact with others, and your self-image as well.

---

1. Describe your initial feelings around witnessing (watching videos or hearing about) the murder of unarmed black folk.

2. How have you traditionally coped after experiencing these traumatic events?

3. What do you think the long-term and continued impact of this trauma has been in your life?

You Good, Bruh?

What emotion(s) are you feeling today? Circle them.

Joyful	Neutral	Anxious
Grateful	Numb	Fearful
Motivated	Sad	Guilty
Hopeful	Tired	Angry
Content	Stressed	Other: __________

Exhale

List up to three reasons (or interactions or thoughts) why you're feeling the emotion(s):

1. ______________________________

2. ______________________________

3. ______________________________

Release Point

Here is today's focus and curated definition.

eq

self-care

/ˌself'ker / *noun*

1. taking steps to maintain and better one's health
2. actively prioritizing one's well-being
3. activities done for the purpose of promoting mental, emotional, and physical health

Make Sure You're *Really* Good First

Being in tune with our emotions as black men also means we know when we need to recharge and take a step back to take care of ourselves. Self-care, or making time and space for yourself and your needs, is integral in ensuring that we are operating from a healthy overflow and not out of depletion. Yet, in the busyness of life, we don't prioritize self-care.

Think through an ideal day for yourself, with a lens of self-care and create a schedule of it in the table below. This day should include things that bring you joy, foster physical, mental, or emotional health, and allow you to rest. *See page 94 if you need suggestions.*

Self-Care Day Schedule

Try to fill in 1-2 things you can do at each part of the day. Feel free to add specific times for each activity.

Time of Day	Activities
Morning	
Afternoon	
Evening	

Challenge: Make this day happen within the next week! You should also regularly commit to it. You can make it a weekly, bi-monthly, or monthly occurrence.

day nineteen

You Good, Bruh?

What emotion(s) are you feeling today? Circle them.

Joyful	Neutral	Anxious
Grateful	Numb	Fearful
Motivated	Sad	Guilty
Hopeful	Tired	Angry
Content	Stressed	Other: __________

Exhale

List up to three reasons (or interactions or thoughts) why you're feeling the emotion(s):

1. ______________________________

2. ______________________________

3. ______________________________

Release Point

Here is today's focus and curated definition.

self

laughter

/ ˈlaftər/ *noun*

1. the sound of amusement
2. a sign of joy
3. a contagious emotion

laughter

The Best Medicine

In my first year in the classroom, I was being observed by my administration for the first time. Obviously, this was extremely nerve-wracking for me, especially considering that my first year was rough. As I was teaching and trying to make the best impression possible, I tripped over my projector's power supply cord. With the little finesse I had, I caught myself before faceplanting. My kids, however, were struggling to hold it together. One of my students yelled out, "Aw mane, Mr. Steele, you aight?!" I ignored him and continued with class, but I definitely saw my administrators at the back holding back their laughter.

I can look back on this and laugh, seeing it as one of the bright spots in a season that was particularly dark for me. Laughter is joy actualized. Laughter helps us remember that not all is bad in our lives. In a moment of laughter, we are able to, even if just for an instant, release ourselves from all that tries to get us down. And, who better to laugh at than yourself?

Hopefully, you will actually laugh while writing today's journal entry. There are some really heavy points in this journey, so embrace this light moment.

---

1. Describe your funniest and/or most embarrassing moment in your life thus far. Write as though you are telling the story to your friends. Use as many details as possible.

2. How does it feel to recount this moment?

day twenty

You Good, Bruh?

What emotion(s) are you feeling today? Circle them.

Joyful	Neutral	Anxious
Grateful	Numb	Fearful
Motivated	Sad	Guilty
Hopeful	Tired	Angry
Content	Stressed	Other: __________

Exhale

List up to three reasons (or interactions or thoughts) why you're feeling the emotion(s):

1. ______________________________

2. ______________________________

3. ______________________________

Release Point

Here is today's focus and curated definition.

identity

assimilation

/ əˌsimiˈlāSH(ə)n/ *noun*

1. adjusting to a dominant culture
2. lessening self in favor of what is deemed acceptable
3. acquiring mainstream habits, behaviors, and mannerism to avoid marginalization

The Obama Effect

One thing President Obama does effectively is code-switch: adjusting his mannerisms and the way he talks according to his audience. The difference in his interactions with black folks and white folks received a ton of attention while he was in office.

As a black man, you probably have learned the art of code-switching. We often have to operate in spaces and institutions that were not built for us; spaces that dampen, or even silence the way that we show up and present ourselves in them. Though such adjustment seems normal, it leads us to find undue comfort in living inauthentically.

The purpose of today's entry is to think about the ways your true self is being compromised. From there, make a commitment to show up in your full self as much as you can. You'll see that, in most cases, the cost of inauthenticity far outweighs the risk of not being yourself.

---

1. When and where do you feel you have to code-switch most often?

2. How does it feel to have to be inauthentic in these spaces?

3. What do you think the risk is if you showed up as your true, uninhibited self in those spaces?

4. What do you need to be true to show-up as your authentic self more often?

You Good, Bruh?

What emotion(s) are you feeling today? Circle them.

Joyful	Neutral	Anxious
Grateful	Numb	Fearful
Motivated	Sad	Guilty
Hopeful	Tired	Angry
Content	Stressed	Other: __________

Exhale

List up to three reasons (or interactions or thoughts) why you're feeling the emotion(s):

1. ______________________________

2. ______________________________

3. ______________________________

Release Point

Here is today's focus and curated definition.

eq

tears

/ tir / noun

1. clear liquid that comes from eye when one is crying
2. a form of emotional cleansing
3. your body's natural way of responding to its experiences

Real Men Cry

Tears are your body's natural self-healing mechanism. However, we are taught that men shouldn't cry, or emote in any way that violates arbitrary rules of masculinity. By trying to uphold these expectations, we have blocked a major channel of release, relief, and restoration. Brother, you cannot be emotionally healthy if you have parameters around how you "acceptably" express emotions.

Today, we are going to begin the work of deconstructing those expectations that have been preventing you from crying as you should. The questions below focus on past experiences but allow them to be a motivator to emote differently in the future.

---

1. When's the last time you wanted to cry but did not cry?

2. Why didn't you cry?

3. What do you think the impact would have been if you did cry?

You Good, Bruh?

What emotion(s) are you feeling today? Circle them.

Joyful	Neutral	Anxious
Grateful	Numb	Fearful
Motivated	Sad	Guilty
Hopeful	Tired	Angry
Content	Stressed	Other: ________

Exhale

List up to three reasons (or interactions or thoughts) why you're feeling the emotion(s):

1. ________________________________

2. ________________________________

3. ________________________________

Release Point

Here is today's focus and curated definition.

self

regret

/ rə'gret/ noun

1. a negative emotion associated with something that has occurred and been done
2. a source of anguish, due to a sense of fault
3. an emotion that prevents one from future risks

You Are More Than That

You are more than your latest mess-up or biggest regret, brother. Your worth is not reduced because of your past. We all have regrets: mistakes made, opportunities missed, loved ones hurt. The issue with regrets is that they hold us back. They prevent us from taking risks, accepting new opportunities, and repairing or developing relationships.

The first steps to moving forward beyond these regrets are acknowledgment and letting go. Let's walk through the beginning of that process today.

---

1. What's that one mistake, thing you did, or other regret that continues to bother you?

2. How does holding onto this regret continue to affect you? How has it stopped you from moving forward?

3. In the box below, write a simple apology to yourself for that regret. Be specific about the things you are continuing to hold onto.

Now, read the apology aloud and forgive yourself – literally. Accept your apology in third person.

4. List any additional steps you need to take to let this regret go (i.e. asking someone for forgiveness, telling someone the truth, etc.)

____

____

____

____

5. Make a commitment to yourself on when you will do these items.

I will complete these items to let go of my regrets and catalyze my forward momentum by ____________________.
(insert date)

You Good, Bruh?

What emotion(s) are you feeling today? Circle them.

Joyful	Neutral	Anxious
Grateful	Numb	Fearful
Motivated	Sad	Guilty
Hopeful	Tired	Angry
Content	Stressed	Other: ________

Exhale

List up to three reasons (or interactions or thoughts) why you're feeling the emotion(s):

1. ______________________________

2. ______________________________

3. ______________________________

Release Point

Here is today's focus and curated definition.

Identity

freedom

/ 'frēdəm/ *noun*

1. no longer subject to
2. a state of liberation
3. no longer enslaved or imprisoned

Broken Chains

Black masculinity, or being a black man, can feel like it comes with a particular set of limitations for when, where, and how you enter the world. Truthfully, these unspoken rules of engagement are two-fold: one set for society in general, and another set within the black community. If you find your own presentation of black masculinity even remotely deviant from either of these constraints set by the gatekeepers of each realm, it can feel like your existence is at times untenable.

This entry is about creating space for yourself to show up as you please. Embrace the confusion that may swell as you read the question. We are so used to a way of being that keeps us safe and accepted that reimagining a different way of being may feel odd. Spend extra time with this, if needed. There is intentionally little guidance today. Feel free to use phrases, lists, drawings, symbols, or whatever best represents your glimpse of freedom.

If the bounds of black masculinity didn't exist, what would you be free to do? How would you show up?

day twenty-four

You Good, Bruh?

What emotion(s) are you feeling today? Circle them.

Joyful	Neutral	Anxious
Grateful	Numb	Fearful
Motivated	Sad	Guilty
Hopeful	Tired	Angry
Content	Stressed	Other: __________

Exhale

List up to three reasons (or interactions or thoughts) why you're feeling the emotion(s):

1. ______________________________

2. ______________________________

3. ______________________________

Release Point

Here is today's focus and curated definition.

eq

wholeness

/ ˈhōlnəs/ *noun*

1. in good physical, emotional, and mental health
2. being undamaged
3. being well in mind, body, and spirit

Live Well

A car only runs at maximum potential if all of its parts are taken care of and routinely serviced. One routine service you should get on your car is an alignment. Maintaining proper alignment on a car ensures fuel efficiency, smooth-riding, safe driving, and many other benefits. It can be said that without being in alignment, a car won't continue to function well.

Brother, you are a complex masterpiece; even more so than a car. You also need to remain in alignment, a characteristic that fosters wholeness. The quality of wholeness can only be achieved by taking care of all aspects of your humanity. One way to think about this is the alignment of your mind, body, and spirt. If any one of these is not being nourished, your holistic health is compromised.

Use the diagram on the next page to fill in the ways you currently nourish your mind, body, and spirit, and then answer the questions that follow. Here is some guidance on the three aspects:

Mind: This includes your mental and emotional health, capacity for learning, and quest for knowledge. Nourishing this could look like doing activities that are mentally stimulating and seeing a therapist.

Body: This includes your physical health and activity. Nourishing this could look like healthy eating and sleeping habits as well as staying active.

Spirit: This includes your faith, spirituality, and sense of morality. Nourishing this could look like active religious practice or taking space to connect to a being higher than yourself.

What do you do to nourish your holistic self? (fill in each part)

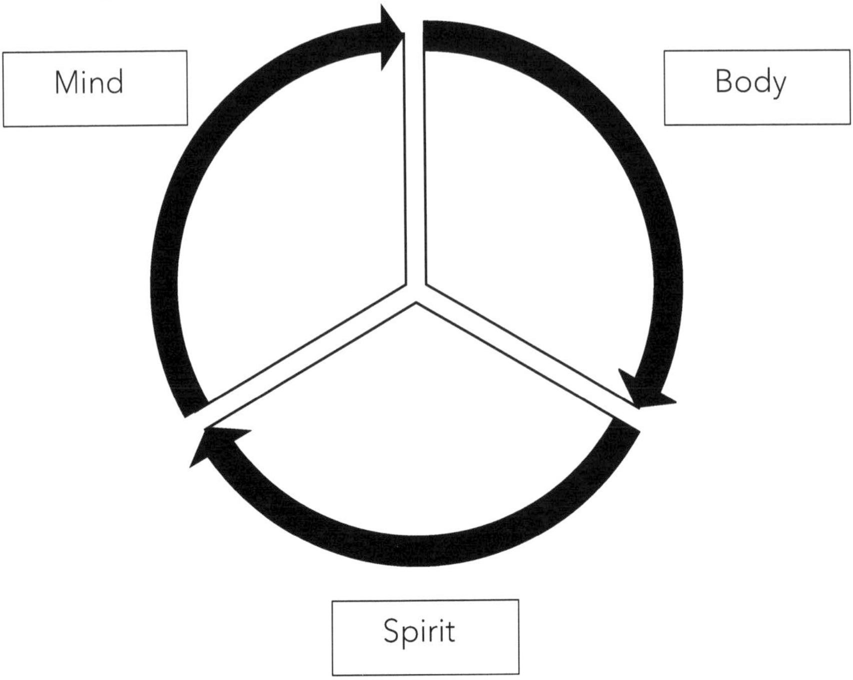

Reflect:

1. Do you feel like your mind, body, and spirit are in alignment? Why or why not?

2. Which aspect receives the most nourishment? The least?

3. What's one way you can nourish your least aligned category this week?

day twenty-five

You Good, Bruh?

What emotion(s) are you feeling today? Circle them.

Joyful	Neutral	Anxious
Grateful	Numb	Fearful
Motivated	Sad	Guilty
Hopeful	Tired	Angry
Content	Stressed	Other: ________

Exhale

List up to three reasons (or interactions or thoughts) why you're feeling the emotion(s):

1. ______________________________

2. ______________________________

3. ______________________________

Release Point

Here is today's focus and curated definition.

self

enlightenment

/ inˈlītnmənt/ *noun*

1. a sense of greater insight
2. awareness that insinuates a change of behavior, attitude, or way of doing things
3. a state of increased knowledge and wisdom

Dear Younger Me

As we begin the last few days of the first part of this journal, we will start to focus more on where you want to go after this journey. Yet, sometimes we get so caught up in becoming a better version of ourselves that our goals seem to be an ever-moving target that only gets further away from us. It can be helpful to reflect on your life to this point. Regardless of your age, you have grown and learned so much to this point. Reflecting on lessons learned is beneficial both to remind yourself of your progress to this point and to motivate you toward more personal development.

Write a letter to a younger version of yourself sharing lessons learned, warnings, and/or the encouragement you needed. Determine the age of your younger self and try to choose an age that is at least ten years younger than your current age. You can determine the tone of this letter. It can be light and funny or more serious and informative. Be sure to be authentic to yourself.

Age: _______

Dear Younger Me,

day twenty-six

You Good, Bruh?

What emotion(s) are you feeling today? Circle them.

Joyful	Neutral	Anxious
Grateful	Numb	Fearful
Motivated	Sad	Guilty
Hopeful	Tired	Angry
Content	Stressed	Other: __________

Exhale

List up to three reasons (or interactions or thoughts) why you're feeling the emotion(s):

1. ____________________

2. ____________________

3. ____________________

Release Point

Here is today's focus and curated definition.

identity

insecurity
/ˌinsəˈkyo͝orədē/ *noun*

1. a source of low self-esteem
2. a critical posture towards a part of oneself
3. a feeling of inferiority

Silence the Inner Critic

Growing up, I was always critical of the way I presented my masculinity. I was not the muscular, emotionally constipated, alpha male that society told me I needed to be. I was the skinny boy who was seen as sensitive by his peers. My inner critic told me that I was "too much" amongst other things, and I spent years of my life trying to fit in the mold. Finally, I realized the pathway to true joy and healing was to silence that inner critic and allow myself to show up in the way that is true to me.

Most people, if not all, have an inner critic. The annoying little person inside us that makes us doubt our worth. Add to that the societal expectations of manhood and the burden of countering the societal stereotypes of black manhood, and the inner critic may seem like he has a megaphone inside of you. Silence that critic today, brother.

In the table below, write down 3-5 phrases that your inner critic repeats to you during the day. Then, take those phrases and rewrite them in an affirming way.

Inner Critic Phrase	Affirm Yourself, Brother
Example: You're too much!	*Your light is needed in the world. The people who are meant to be in your life will accept AND love you!*

Challenge: The next time your inner critic starts rumbling in your head, return to this entry and audibly state your affirmations. Don't let those feelings of inadequacy fester.

day twenty-seven

You Good, Bruh?

What emotion(s) are you feeling today? Circle them.

Joyful	Neutral	Anxious
Grateful	Numb	Fearful
Motivated	Sad	Guilty
Hopeful	Tired	Angry
Content	Stressed	Other: ________

Exhale

List up to three reasons (or interactions or thoughts) why you're feeling the emotion(s):

1. ______________________________

2. ______________________________

3. ______________________________

Release Point

Here is today's focus and curated definition.

eq

safety

/ ˈsāftē/ *noun*

1. protection from harm or danger
2. a feeling of acceptance and welcome
3. an environment or state conducive to letting one's guard down

Safe Place

A part of emotional awareness and intelligence is recognizing environments that give you the freedom to feel and express as you want and need. Moreover, true growth and healing are complemented by coupling your journey with an environment that is safe for you to be the fullest version of yourself; free of the expectations, preconceived notions, and negative vibes of broader society and any other space that isn't conducive to your transformation.

Today, you will explore the parts of your life that are safe spaces for you. Try to think of safety as more than just "comfort." Safe space doesn't mean that the places don't challenge you; rather, they don't expect you to show up as anything other than who you are. This entry may also be a hard realization for you when you put pen to paper on the people and places that don't serve you.

---

1. Where do you feel most safe to be yourself? What about that space engenders safety?

2. Around whom do you feel most comfortable to be yourself? What about those people engender safety?

3. Where or with whom do you feel stifled or unsafe? What about these spaces and people make you feel unsafe?

Challenge: Push yourself to actually make the necessary adjustments in life after this reflection. Your personal development and well-being depend on it.

day twenty-eight

You Good, Bruh?

What emotion(s) are you feeling today? Circle them.

Joyful	Neutral	Anxious
Grateful	Numb	Fearful
Motivated	Sad	Guilty
Hopeful	Tired	Angry
Content	Stressed	Other: ________

Exhale

List up to three reasons (or interactions or thoughts) why you're feeling the emotion(s):

1. ____________________

2. ____________________

3. ____________________

Release Point

Here is today's focus and curated definition.

self

vision

/ ˈviZHən/ *noun*

1. the ability to see
2. a plan for the future utilizing wisdom and imagination
3. a clear way forward or goal for the future

Your Future is in Your Own Hands

The impact of completing the first part of this journal will be fleeting unless you commit to growing from here. This is only the first step, and I hope it motivates you to show up better, live healthier, and own your light. Yet, without direction, your personal development will be aimless and only improve haphazardly. Black man, the world needs you, in all of your uniqueness, to be poised for leadership, contribution, and service.

One way to commit to your growth is to write out a vision for yourself. The act of writing a specific vision represents an important step from idealizing to actualizing. As you answer the question below, think about where you want to be, who you want to be, what goals you want to have accomplished. Make sure to think about this in all aspects of your life: mentally, emotionally, relationally, financially, etc.

---

1. Who will you be and where will you be a year from now? You may write this as a set of goals, a vision statement, or use any other form.

2. Who will you be and where will you be in five years? You may write this as a set of goals, a vision statement, or use any other form.

3. What small change can you make in the near future to start making your vision a reality? What is the change?

Challenge: List the steps you need to take to make that change.

You Good, Bruh?

What emotion(s) are you feeling today? Circle them.

Joyful	Neutral	Anxious
Grateful	Numb	Fearful
Motivated	Sad	Guilty
Hopeful	Tired	Angry
Content	Stressed	Other: ________

Exhale

List up to three reasons (or interactions or thoughts) why you're feeling the emotion(s):

1. ______________________________

2. ______________________________

3. ______________________________

Release Point

Here is today's focus and curated definition.

identity

exemplar

/ igˈzemplər/ *noun*

1. a role model
2. a person with strong characteristics to be emulated
3. an epitomized example

exemplar

The Embodiment of Your Vision

My hope is that upon completing this journal, you will be motivated to do more of the work you need personally toward healing and development into *your* full potential as a black man. On your journey to becoming a better version of you, it is sometimes helpful to pinpoint a sort of role model, or a black man that embodies the qualities you highlighted in your own vision yesterday.

When thinking of your model of black manhood, think about the themes and topics of this journal. Attempt to select someone who pushes beyond the typical expectations of manhood and represents a black man with a more comprehensive understanding of themselves and their emotions. This person can be someone you know, a celebrity, or any man you've admired and want to imitate.

---

1. Who is your role model for black manhood?

2. What qualities do they have that you want to emulate?

Feel free to add any of the qualities you discussed today to your vision from yesterday.

You Good, Bruh?

What emotion(s) are you feeling today? Circle them.

Joyful	Neutral	Anxious
Grateful	Numb	Fearful
Motivated	Sad	Guilty
Hopeful	Tired	Angry
Content	Stressed	Other: ________

Exhale

List up to three reasons (or interactions or thoughts) why you're feeling the emotion(s):

1. ____________________

2. ____________________

3. ____________________

Release Point

Here is today's focus and curated definition.

closure

affirmation

/ ˌafərˈmāSH(ə)n/ *noun*

1. a personal declaration
2. an encouraging phrase
3. of a statement of truth

affirmation

"Show Them Who You Are"

My favorite part in *Black Panther* is when T'Challa fought M'Baku for the right to be Black Panther. Just as it seemed like T'Challa was down for the count, his Queen Mother yells, "Show them who you are!" After that phrase, T'Challa, now reminded of the power and strength that ran through his veins, mustered up the energy to defeat M'Baku.

Black man, you have spent a month journaling at this point. Hopefully, you now have a greater awareness of who you are and the light that you carry. Even when you are weighed down by the worries of life or society devalues your existence, I hope you can affirm yourself, and show the world who you *really* are.

Now, for the last day of part one of this journal. I want you to circle back to the first activity of describing yourself. You've asserted who you are, before and now affirm with boldness who you are, brother.

Once you finish your list on the next page, revisit day 4 of this journal and compare. You can use one of the free journal entries to reflect on what was the same or what was different. I hope you see and experience the beginning of healing, growth, and transformation, brother

To give you some inspiration, here are some things I know to be true about you, Black man:

1. You are strong.
2. You are powerful.
3. You are courageous.
4. Your blackness is beautiful.
5. You matter.

Describe YOURSELF, Brother.
TEN AFFIRMATIONS

#1: I AM ______________________________

#2: I AM ______________________________

#3: I AM ______________________________

#4: I AM ______________________________

#5: I AM ______________________________

#6: I AM ______________________________

#7: I AM ______________________________

#8: I AM ______________________________

#9: I AM ______________________________

#10: I AM _____________________________

Sample Values List *
(for use on day 13)
Do not be limited by this list!

Authenticity	Determination	Independence	Recognition
Achievement	Excellence	Justice	Resilience
Adventure	Family	Knowledge	Security
Balance	Friendship	Loyalty	Spirituality
Challenge	Growth	Mindfulness	Success
Community	Honesty	Optimism	Thankfulness
Creativity	Humor	Passion	Wealth

*adapted from TapRoot (http://www.taproot.com/archives/37771)

Sample Self-Care Activities
(for use on day 18)

Sleeping in	Seeing a therapist	Journaling
Working out	Meditation/Prayer	Reading self-development books
Participating in a hobby	Getting a massage	Trying something new
Spending time with family	Hiking/Nature Experience	Solo vacation
Connecting with friends/community	Screen-free time	Spending time with God/other Higher Power

part two

self-directed journal.

Now that you have finished the first part of this journal, part two will give you more freedom to write about what's on your mind and heart. The first part was meant to get you into the practice of journaling, but this part is meant for you to have the autonomy to express yourself as authentically as possible over the next 14 days. Here's to YOUR journey and YOUR story, brother.

If you find yourself having difficulty writing at any point, you can use this space to elaborate on any activity from the first part or use the questions below as a starting point.

on self:

1. What does success mean to you?
2. What would your friends, family, or community say are your best qualities?
3. What is your life's mantra? Why?
4. Where or in whom do you place your faith? How does that sustain your hope amongst life's troubles?
5. Plan the biopic of your life. Describe the actors, general plot, theme, and anything else you would want to include.

on identity:

1. How do the other parts of your identity intersect with and affect the presentation of your black masculinity?
2. Has your black masculinity, or any part of your identity, ever felt invisible? Explain.
3. What privileges does your black manhood afford you?
4. What affirms your identity?
5. What do you want your legacy to be after you die?

on eq:

1. What stresses you out?
2. Do you struggle to explain your feelings to other people? Why or why not?
3. What or who gives you life? What/who gives you energy?
4. How do you express your love? How do you prefer to receive it?
5. What brings you peace?

You Good, Bruh?

What emotion(s) are you feeling today? Circle them.

Joyful	Neutral	Anxious
Grateful	Numb	Fearful
Motivated	Sad	Guilty
Hopeful	Tired	Angry
Content	Stressed	Other: ________

Exhale

Talk about the emotion(s), use one of the prompts at the beginning of part two to get you started, or talk about whatever else is on your mind today...

You Good, Bruh?

What emotion(s) are you feeling today? Circle them.

Joyful	Neutral	Anxious
Grateful	Numb	Fearful
Motivated	Sad	Guilty
Hopeful	Tired	Angry
Content	Stressed	Other: ________

Exhale

Talk about the emotion(s), use one of the prompts at the beginning of part two to get you started, or talk about whatever else is on your mind today...

You Good, Bruh?

What emotion(s) are you feeling today? Circle them.

Joyful	Neutral	Anxious
Grateful	Numb	Fearful
Motivated	Sad	Guilty
Hopeful	Tired	Angry
Content	Stressed	Other: __________

Exhale

Talk about the emotion(s), use one of the prompts at the beginning of part two to get you started, or talk about whatever else is on your mind today...

You Good, Bruh?

What emotion(s) are you feeling today? Circle them.

Joyful	Neutral	Anxious
Grateful	Numb	Fearful
Motivated	Sad	Guilty
Hopeful	Tired	Angry
Content	Stressed	Other: ________

Exhale

Talk about the emotion(s), use one of the prompts at the beginning of part two to get you started, or talk about whatever else is on your mind today...

You Good, Bruh?

What emotion(s) are you feeling today? Circle them.

Joyful	Neutral	Anxious
Grateful	Numb	Fearful
Motivated	Sad	Guilty
Hopeful	Tired	Angry
Content	Stressed	Other: ___________

Exhale

Talk about the emotion(s), use one of the prompts at the beginning of part two to get you started, or talk about whatever else is on your mind today...

day thirty-six

You Good, Bruh?

What emotion(s) are you feeling today? Circle them.

Joyful	Neutral	Anxious
Grateful	Numb	Fearful
Motivated	Sad	Guilty
Hopeful	Tired	Angry
Content	Stressed	Other: ___________

Exhale

Talk about the emotion(s), use one of the prompts at the beginning of part two to get you started, or talk about whatever else is on your mind today...

day thirty-seven

You Good, Bruh?

What emotion(s) are you feeling today? Circle them.

Joyful	Neutral	Anxious
Grateful	Numb	Fearful
Motivated	Sad	Guilty
Hopeful	Tired	Angry
Content	Stressed	Other: ___________

Exhale

Talk about the emotion(s), use one of the prompts at the beginning of part two to get you started, or talk about whatever else is on your mind today...

day thirty-eight

You Good, Bruh?

What emotion(s) are you feeling today? Circle them.

Joyful	Neutral	Anxious
Grateful	Numb	Fearful
Motivated	Sad	Guilty
Hopeful	Tired	Angry
Content	Stressed	Other: __________

Exhale

Talk about the emotion(s), use one of the prompts at the beginning of part two to get you started, or talk about whatever else is on your mind today...

day thirty-nine

You Good, Bruh?

What emotion(s) are you feeling today? Circle them.

Joyful	Neutral	Anxious
Grateful	Numb	Fearful
Motivated	Sad	Guilty
Hopeful	Tired	Angry
Content	Stressed	Other: __________

Exhale

Talk about the emotion(s), use one of the prompts at the beginning of part two to get you started, or talk about whatever else is on your mind today...

day forty

You Good, Bruh?

What emotion(s) are you feeling today? Circle them.

Joyful	Neutral	Anxious
Grateful	Numb	Fearful
Motivated	Sad	Guilty
Hopeful	Tired	Angry
Content	Stressed	Other: ________

Exhale

Talk about the emotion(s), use one of the prompts at the beginning of part two to get you started, or talk about whatever else is on your mind today...

day forty-one

You Good, Bruh?

What emotion(s) are you feeling today? Circle them.

Joyful	Neutral	Anxious
Grateful	Numb	Fearful
Motivated	Sad	Guilty
Hopeful	Tired	Angry
Content	Stressed	Other: ________

Exhale

Talk about the emotion(s), use one of the prompts at the beginning of part two to get you started, or talk about whatever else is on your mind today...

You Good, Bruh?

What emotion(s) are you feeling today? Circle them.

Joyful	Neutral	Anxious
Grateful	Numb	Fearful
Motivated	Sad	Guilty
Hopeful	Tired	Angry
Content	Stressed	Other: ________

Exhale

Talk about the emotion(s), use one of the prompts at the beginning of part two to get you started, or talk about whatever else is on your mind today...

You Good, Bruh?

What emotion(s) are you feeling today? Circle them.

Joyful	Neutral	Anxious
Grateful	Numb	Fearful
Motivated	Sad	Guilty
Hopeful	Tired	Angry
Content	Stressed	Other: ________

Exhale

Talk about the emotion(s), use one of the prompts at the beginning of part two to get you started, or talk about whatever else is on your mind today...

You Good, Bruh?

What emotion(s) are you feeling today? Circle them.

Joyful	Neutral	Anxious
Grateful	Numb	Fearful
Motivated	Sad	Guilty
Hopeful	Tired	Angry
Content	Stressed	Other: __________

Exhale

Talk about the emotion(s), use one of the prompts at the beginning of part two to get you started, or talk about whatever else is on your mind today...

part three

your story. your narrative.

The final step of this journey is all about space. Space for you to breathe. Space for you to reflect. Space for you to write your story.

So, write your story, brother. In your time. In your way. In your words.

Because all that you have and all that you are matters.

Go forth and write, brother.

day forty-five

You Good, Bruh?

What emotion(s) are you feeling today? Circle them.

Joyful	Neutral	Anxious
Grateful	Numb	Fearful
Motivated	Sad	Guilty
Hopeful	Tired	Angry
Content	Stressed	Other: __________

Release Point

This is the last day of this journal. Write the narrative of your story, your way. You have been able to explore many parts of yourself on this journey, so you should have a better understanding of who you are. You can use the prompts from the first part of this journal and anything else you've written since then as inspiration. Own your story, brother.

fin.

If you made it to this point, I hope you celebrate yourself. This journey was likely not always an easy task and may have been hard to stay motivated to complete. But you did it. Salute, bother.

This is only the beginning though. Continue to make space in your life for this personal development, reflection, and healing.

Buy another journal and keep writing.

See a therapist.

Invest in community.

Show up authentically.

Remove the things in your life that don't serve you or your purpose.

Work to understand your story and its impacts more.

And most of all, never stop breathing.

Yours in brotherhood,
-B. Steele

Made in the USA
Columbia, SC
02 February 2022

55287351R00083